THE
NAVAJO
INDIANS

THE JUNIOR LIBRARY OF
AMERICAN INDIANS

THE
NAVAJO
INDIANS

Leigh Hope Wood

CHELSEA HOUSE PUBLISHERS
New York   Philadelphia

FRONTISPIECE: A Navajo silversmith, photographed in 1915

CHAPTER TITLE ORNAMENT: An illustration of a goddess, based on an image in a Navajo sandpainting

Chelsea House Publishers
EDITOR-IN-CHIEF   Remmel Nunn
MANAGING EDITOR   Karyn Gullen Browne
COPY CHIEF   Juliann Barbato
PICTURE EDITOR   Adrian G. Allen
ART DIRECTOR   Maria Epes
DEPUTY COPY CHIEF   Mark Rifkin
ASSISTANT ART DIRECTOR   Noreen Romano
MANUFACTURING MANAGER   Gerald Levine
SYSTEMS MANAGER   Lindsey Ottman
PRODUCTION MANAGER   Joseph Romano
PRODUCTION COORDINATOR   Marie Claire Cebrián

The Junior Library of American Indians
SENIOR EDITOR   Liz Sonneborn

Staff for THE NAVAJO INDIANS
COPY EDITOR   Laurie Kahn
EDITORIAL ASSISTANT   Michele Haddad
DESIGNER   Debora Smith
PICTURE RESEARCHER   Sandy Jones
COVER ILLUSTRATOR   Vilma Ortiz

3 5 7 9 8 6 4 2

Library of Congress Cataloging-in-Publication Data

Wood, Leigh Hope.
   The Navajo Indians/by Leigh Hope Wood.
      p.   cm.—(The Junior library of American Indians)
   Includes index.
   Summary: Examines the history, culture, and future prospects of the Navajo Indians.
   ISBN 0-7910-1651-X
   1. Navajo Indians—Juvenile literature. [1. Navajo Indians.
2. Indians of North America.] I. Title. II. Series.
                                                          90-24821
E99.N3W747 1991   CIP
970.004'972—dc20   AC

CONTENTS

The Fourth World,
*by Navajo artist
Andy Tsinajinnie*

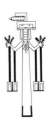

CHAPTER **1**

Creating the Navajos

Before humans learned to write about the world and their adventures in it, they shared their experiences by telling stories. People, especially children, have always enjoyed listening to storytellers. So, many tales have been remembered and told again and again over the ages. In this way, people have learned of their history, and the past has not been forgotten.

For the Navajo Indians, the stories handed down to them by their ancestors are still very important. The tales express what the Navajos value and believe. They teach the Navajos the proper way to behave and help them understand the meaning of their ceremonies. They also describe the four sacred mountains surrounding the Navajo homeland, which was located in parts of what are now Arizona, New Mexico, Colorado, and Utah.

In sum, these stories make up the *mythology* of the Navajo people. As a set of stories relating historical events, mythology helps to explain the growth of a particular society. It deals with the creation of a world, the development of a way of life.

To other groups of people, who have their own various mythologies, the stories told by the Navajos may seem too unfamiliar to believe. People are most familiar with their own world and their own way of life. Yet, by listening to stories such as the one of the Navajo creation, people can learn much about other societies.

The Navajo Indians believe that their ancestors journeyed through three different worlds before coming to the Glittering World, the place in which the Navajos presently live. The first was the Black World. Here, the white cloud and the black cloud met, causing First Man and a perfect ear of white corn to be formed. First Woman, turquoise, white shell, and a perfect ear of yellow corn were also created here when the yellow cloud and the blue cloud met.

Many animals lived in this world with First Man and First Woman. Except for the Insect Beings, all the animals fought amongst themselves. The other beings had not learned to act as a group, so they quarreled. The Insects, however, lived in harmony. They listened to each other and sought one another's approval before taking any action.

Because all living things were not able to live in harmony in the Black World, First Woman, First Man, and all of the animals moved upward into the Blue World. Here lived many other animals. There were Blue Hawks, Blue Jays, Wolves, Mountain Lions, and Insects larger than those from the Black World.

Once again, everyone began to quarrel. So, First Man performed ceremonies that allowed them to move to the Yellow World. In this world, there were six mountains and many more animals, such as Squirrels, Deer, and Snakes.

Among the animals who traveled to the Yellow World was Coyote. He was a trickster, and his jokes always caused problems for others. When Coyote arrived in the Yellow World with First Man and First Woman, he asked them for a piece of white shell. He took this white shell to the river, and the water began to rise and fall. A flood threatened to swallow the Yellow World, so First Man planted a female reed. Through the reed's hollow center, all beings climbed up into the Glittering World.

In this bright place, First Man and First Woman formed the four sacred mountains. Their world took shape. The stars were put into the sky. The sun and moon were formed. Day and night were created. Then, when the seasons were chosen, the first crops were harvested.

One morning at dawn, after arriving at Huerfano Mountain, First Man and First Woman heard a baby cry. They found an infant girl in Gobernador Canyon, born from the mingling of darkness and dawn. First Man and First Woman took care of the child and named her Changing Woman.

Before she left childhood, Changing Woman was given a ceremony, called the *kinaalda,* so that she could walk in beauty as an adult. Sometime after her kinaalda, she fell asleep by a waterfall and was visited by the Sun. Soon after, she gave birth to twin sons. She named the two boys Child Born of Water and Monster Slayer. They became hunters and grew up to be very strong.

While the twins were still children, Changing Woman created the corn plant.

Later, she mixed cornmeal with scrapings of her own skin and used this mixture to make the first Navajo people. The Glittering World was not safe for the Navajos, however, because it was filled with monsters. To help the people, Child Born of Water and Monster Slayer set out to kill the monsters.

One day while they were hunting, the two boys saw a small hole in the ground. From the hole arose a voice that urged the boys to come inside. The hole grew larger,

Sun God and His Wife, painted by Navajo artist Gerald Nailor in 1938

and the twins entered. Once inside, they met Spider Woman, and they asked her if she knew who their father was. She told them that she could help them find their father and that he would be able to assist them in killing the monsters. Spider Woman warned the boys that the trip would be dangerous, and she helped prepare them for it.

On their journey, the twins survived many trials. They managed to get past sharp reeds that could have cut them to pieces. They crossed sands that could have shifted and smothered them. They sneaked through a canyon that could have crushed them. Then they avoided four rock columns that had the power to turn them into old men.

When they arrived at the Sun's home, they found that the house was guarded by the Great Snake, the Black Bear, the Big Thunder, and the Big Wind. They chanted prayers that Spider Woman had taught them to get past these guards. Inside the house, the boys met the Sun for the first time.

The Sun, however, refused to admit that he was their father. So, the boys took a dangerous test to prove themselves. The Sun threw them against white spikes in the eastern wall of his house, but the boys were not hurt. Then he threw them against spikes of turquoise in the southern wall, against the yellow spikes in the western wall, and against the spikes of black rock in the northern wall. The boys were still uninjured. The Sun then invited them to smoke tobacco from his turquoise pipe. This tobacco was so strong it usually killed anyone who smoked it. The boys, however, were not harmed by the smoke.

After the boys passed this test, the Sun rewarded them. To Monster Slayer, the Sun gave Lightning That Strikes Crooked. To Child Born of Water, he bestowed Lightning That Flashes Straight. With these weapons the boys were able to kill all the monsters, except for those that cause old age, hunger, lice, and death. So, thanks to Spider Woman and Changing Woman's sons, the Glittering World became safe for the Navajo people.

Navajo storytellers continue to recount the events of their people's creation. The story that they present, however, changes with every telling depending upon the storyteller, the audience, and the event at which it is told. Because it is a boundless tale, a storyteller may choose to include a particular incident in one telling and then leave it out of another.

·TRADITIONAL NAVAJO TERRITORY·

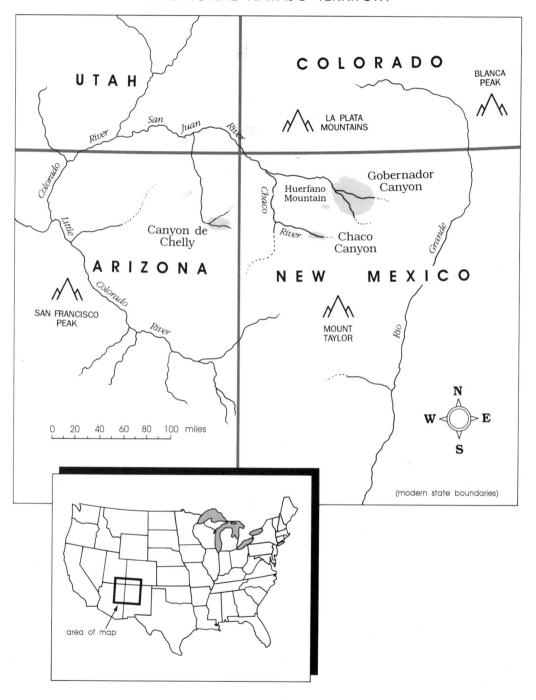

UTAH

COLORADO

BLANCA PEAK

LA PLATA MOUNTAINS

San Juan River

Colorado

Little

Canyon de Chelly

Chaco

Gobernador Canyon

Huerfano Mountain

Chaco Canyon

River

ARIZONA

NEW MEXICO

Grande

Colorado

River

SAN FRANCISCO PEAK

MOUNT TAYLOR

Rio

0 20 40 60 80 100 miles

N
W—◇—E
S

(modern state boundaries)

area of map

The version of the Navajo creation story presented here is one of many, and it provides several specific lessons. It teaches its listeners that humans are not superior to other forms of life, such as insects or snakes. People coexist with animals. The story also stresses the importance of harmony within a group of people. To maintain harmony, change is sometimes necessary.

The Navajos have undergone many changes through the years. A great number have come about through contact with other people—both Indians and non-Indians. In many ways, however, their life has stayed the same. They still live on land surrounded by the four sacred mountains, which are now known as San Francisco Peak, Mount Taylor, Blanca Peak, and La Plata Mountains. Also, many people still speak the Navajo language, practice Navajo ceremonies, and honor the old values. Through centuries of both maintaining a traditional way of life and adapting to changing conditions, they have emerged as the largest Indian tribe in the United States. ▲

Navajo women at work, weaving a blanket on a loom

CHAPTER **2**

The People's Way of Life

The Navajos have not always been a large and powerful Indian group. It took centuries for them to unite and to think of themselves as one people, or tribe. The Navajos became bound together because, over time, they came to have several important things in common. They shared the same land and learned to use its resources in similar ways. They developed a special form of government. Perhaps most importantly, they created their own *culture*.

Culture is the way of life of a group of people—their own special beliefs, ceremonies, and behaviors. The Navajo culture began to take shape hundreds of years ago, long before the United States existed as a nation.

Some scientists believe that about 2,000 years ago the Navajos were living in what is now northwestern Canada and Alaska. In this region, the Navajos lived in loosely organized groups. These groups traveled from place to place, hunting elk, caribou, and other wild animals with bows and arrows. They also fished and gathered berries for food. For housing, they propped up an animal hide with a pole to make a one-room living space.

At some point, the Navajos journeyed south. By about 500 years ago, they be-came residents of what is now the American Southwest. They called themselves Diné (the People), and they called their new home Dinétah (the Land of the People). Here, they had to adapt to many new things.

In the Southwest, wild game was not as plentiful as it had been up north. To feed themselves, the Navajos had to learn to farm. Their teachers were the Pueblo Indi-ans. When the Navajos arrived in the South-west, the Pueblos had been in the area for about 900 years. The land was very dry, and the Pueblos had discovered how to farm us-ing very little water.

In order to tend their fields, the Navajos had to stay in one location for a long time. So, they gave up their old, portable animal homes. Instead, they began building one-room houses from the earth called *hogans*. A hogan was a cone-shaped frame made of logs and bark and covered with mud. A doorway was left in the wall on the east side, so that the sun would shine into the hogan in the morning.

The Navajos lived in small communities spread over a wide territory. Members of the same family tended to live close by, which made it easier for them to work together. The Navajos were up before sunrise. Even children went out with their elders and learned how to work with others. Boys would hunt and track game, and their elders taught them about ceremonies. Girls learned to cook and weave. All children were expected to contribute to the group.

The Navajo people did not have a single leader. Sometimes, though, a leader from a particular area was chosen to tell others about the needs of one community or to lead the Navajos into battle. For day-to-day matters, an older woman was chosen to set the rules for all the people living within each group of hogans. People had to mind their

manners. If someone misbehaved, it reflected badly on the whole family.

All Navajos belonged to a *clan*. A clan is a large group of relatives who have a common ancestor. In traditional Navajo society, husbands and wives were members of different clans, because the Navajos believed it was unhealthy to marry within a clan. The children, too, belonged to only one clan, their mother's.

When a woman and man married, they built their hogan near the wife's mother. A Navajo mother and her child shared a very strong bond. Because of this, a husband, living so near his mother-in-law, could have a difficult time. So in traditional Navajo society, a man tried never to speak to his wife's mother. He tried not to even look at her.

The Navajos valued harmony, happiness, beauty, and goodness. One Navajo word, *hozho*, meant all of these things and much more. In a way, hozho was a type of religion. The Navajos believed that hozho was difficult to maintain because the world has both good and evil elements. All people can be influenced by evil things. So, bad

A Navajo family
outside their hogan
in 1914

things have to be controlled. To help people overcome evil and restore hozho, singers performed ceremonies, called *chantways*.

Singers acted as both priests and doctors. They used chantways as a kind of medicine. When a ceremony was performed to help cure sickness, a *drypainting* (also called a sandpainting) was made. A drypainting is a picture formed on the ground with crushed charcoal and powders of white, yellow, and red sandstone. During a ceremony, the singer moistened his or her hands and placed them on the drypainting, then placed them on the patient's body. This linked the patient to the sacred figures depicted in the drypainting. After the ceremony, the rest of the painting was destroyed, for it was no longer of use.

Some ceremonies were meant to protect people from evil and to promote hozho. One example of this type of ceremony was the *Blessingway rite*. It was performed to protect livestock, to bless a new marriage, to help a woman in childbirth, to protect a warrior from his enemies, and to do many other things. The kinaalda, the ceremony performed for Changing Woman, was one version of the Blessingway rite. It is still performed for Navajo girls when they reach puberty.

A Navajo man creates a drypainting from powdered sandstone and charcoal, 1954.

Like their ancestors of long ago, the Navajos of today perform ceremonies and maintain close ties with family members. Their way of living, though, has always undergone change. Many of the greatest changes occurred after the Navajos came into contact with people from the other side of the world.

Near the end of the 15th century, Spain's Queen Isabella I gave an Italian explorer the money he needed to search for a new trade route to China. Because of her generosity, Christopher Columbus was able to set sail in 1492. By accident, though, he sailed to the Americas, a world never before known to Europeans.

The Spanish people were the first Europeans to travel to the Americas with the intention of settling. Explorers, traders, settlers, and missionaries went to the areas now known as Mexico, South America, and the western United States. To their new home, they brought their own language, religion, dress, housing, and system of government. Once there, they tried to convert the Indians to the Spanish way of life.

A young Navajo girl watches over a flock of sheep in 1915.

At first, Spanish things rather than Spanish ideas had the greatest effect on the Navajos. From Europe, the Spaniards brought horses, cattle, and sheep. By the 18th century, raising sheep had become very important to the Navajo way of life. Almost everybody owned at least a few sheep. All of the Navajos' sheep were kept together in one big herd. People recognized their own sheep simply by sight.

Sheep were important to the Navajos for many reasons. Parents gave lambs to their children to teach them how to raise animals. This helped introduce children to work.

The women used wool from sheep to make yarn, which they wove into blankets for their family. They discovered that some plants could be used to make dyes. With the dyes, women colored their yarn to create blankets with beautiful, bold designs.

Sheep were also a source of meat for the Navajos. Mutton, the meat from older sheep, was not very tasty. The Navajos usually combined mutton with vegetables to make a stew.

The Navajos often gave their sheep away, sometimes as a gift and sometimes as a form of payment. For performing at a ceremony, a singer might receive either

meat or a live sheep. The Navajos believed that rewarding the singer for his or her performance was necessary for a ceremony to be successful, because good things did not come free.

By the 18th century, horses were also very important to the Navajo way of life. On horseback, the Navajos were able to move around more easily and graze their sheep over a wider area of land. They were also able to raid the settlements of Spaniards and other Indians for food. Of course, horses enabled other Indians to raid the Navajos' communities as well.

When Spanish missionaries came to settle in the Southwest, they brought peaches, potatoes, and wheat with them. They also offered the Indians a new religion—Christianity. The Navajos learned how to grow the new vegetables and fruits, but they did not change their spiritual beliefs. Very few were baptized in the Catholic church. If the missionaries tried to force them to attend mass, the Navajos moved a little farther away to live.

Avoiding the Spanish was not as easy for the Pueblo Indians. The Pueblos lived in villages in houses made of stone, so it was difficult for them to move around. They were often forced to attend mass, to work for

Spanish settlers, and to follow Spanish rules. Angered by their treatment, the Pueblos rebelled and drove the Spanish south in 1680. In time, the Spanish returned, though. Some Pueblos then went to live among the Navajos.

The Pueblos and Navajos probably learned much from each other. It is difficult to determine which elements of today's Navajo culture were originally Pueblo. However, it is known that the Pueblos introduced the Navajos to corn.

In the early 18th century, corn became very important to Navajo culture. It was not only a food but a symbol of fertility and prosperity. It even became an element within the Navajos' story of creation. Planting corn was associated with the Navajos' origin, and the growth of the stalk was likened to the growth of the Navajo people.

Their contact with other people in the 17th and 18th centuries surely helped to shape Navajo culture into what it is today. Just as a stalk of corn grows and grows with time, the Navajos continued to prosper as they learned to live with the new groups of people they met. Yet more change was still to come. In the 19th century, some of these changes threatened to tear the stalk from the land and uproot the Navajo people. ▲

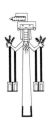

CHAPTER **3**

The Uprooted Come Home

While the Navajos prospered within the four sacred mountains, non-Indians in North America were developing into their own nations. In the late 18th century, settlers from England founded the United States of America. In the early 19th century, descendants of the first Spanish settlers established the nation of Mexico.

At the time, Mexico extended to parts of what is now the southwestern United States. Most of the people living there were Indians. Even though their ancestors had occupied the land for centuries, the Mexicans ignored the Indians' right to the area. The American government agreed that the land did not belong to the Indians, but they

29

discounted Mexico's claim as well. The United States declared that it owned the territory and went to war with Mexico to gain control of it.

The conflict, known as the Mexican War, ended on February 2, 1848. On this date, Mexico and the United States signed the Treaty of Guadalupe Hidalgo. Having lost the war, Mexico was forced to give up territory that included much of present-day Texas, New Mexico, Arizona, Colorado, Utah, Nevada, and California. The Navajo homeland was part of this vast area.

On August 31, 1849, two U.S. representatives and some soldiers traveled to Navajo country. They were sent to hold a conference with a group of Navajos to explain the government's plans. Soon, the government would build forts and open land to American settlers in its newly acquired territory.

At the conference an argument broke out. A Mexican guide claimed that the Navajos had a horse that had been stolen from him. During the conflict, soldiers shot and killed seven Navajos, including an influential leader named Narbona. The news spread quickly to other Navajos. Many vowed never to trust the U.S. government.

Skirmishes between U.S. troops and the Navajos continued to occur. In April 1860, two Navajo leaders named Manuelito and Barboncito led about a thousand warriors in an attack on a U.S. fort. The Navajos lost the battle. Officials in the U.S. Army then decided to force the Navajos to submit to U.S. authority once and for all.

In the fall of 1862, General James Carleton came up with a plan. He wanted to gather all the Indian peoples in this area and move them to Fort Sumner, a post about 250 miles east of Navajo country. Here, he would establish a *reservation*—a piece of land on which only Indians would live. U.S. troops could watch over the Indians confined to a reservation. Carleton had another reason for forcing the Indians to move. He believed that gold and other precious minerals lay hidden in the land belonging to the Navajos and their Apache neighbors. He wanted to open the area to non-Indian miners.

To head the program, Carleton chose a colonel named Kit Carson. Although Carson thought the plan was unwise, he agreed to help. Within six months, the troops under his command had defeated the Mescalero Apaches and moved them to Fort Sumner.

Then, in the summer of 1863, they marched through the heart of Navajo country. According to stories passed down through the years by Navajos, the soldiers burned cornfields and peach orchards. They poisoned wells and shot livestock. They also shot Navajos.

That winter many Navajos went hungry. Desperate and starving, they started to surrender. By the end of the year, 8,000 Navajos had turned themselves in to the U.S. Army. They were all taken from their land and marched 250 miles away to the Bosque Redondo Reservation at Fort Sumner. This march is known today as the Long Walk.

Navajos still tell the stories of how their people were mistreated on the Long Walk. On this very long journey, old people and children were expected to keep up with everyone else. Women who gave birth on the Long Walk were not allowed enough time to recover. Some people were even shot for resisting the soldiers.

The Navajos were very unhappy at Bosque Redondo. The soil was very poor, and harvests were small. To help, the U.S. government paid some non-Indian businessmen to provide the Navajos with food. These people were dishonest, though. They stole most of the government's mon-

continued on page 41

NAVAJO CRAFTS

After the Navajo Indians came to live in what is now the American Southwest, they discovered crafts that greatly enriched their culture. In the late 17th century, Navajo women began weaving very beautiful blankets on simple wooden looms, a skill they probably learned from the Pueblo Indians. In the early 1850s, Navajo men learned from their Mexican neighbors how to work silver coins into jewelry, belts, and horse bridles.

In time, the Navajos became very skilled at their newfound crafts. They no longer imitated the work of their teachers but used their imagination to create items that were distinctly Navajo. When non-Indians began to show a great interest in Navajo work in the late 19th century, traders encouraged the Navajos to make rugs and jewelry for barter. At the trading post, Navajos could exchange these items for non-Indian goods such as cotton fabrics and flour. Weaving and the crafting of silver soon became vital to the Navajo economy.

Silversmiths and weavers still produce highly valued items. Perhaps more important to their culture, however, these crafts remain symbols of Navajo tradition.

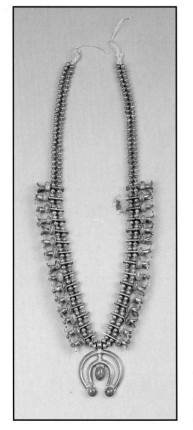

A silver necklace inlaid with turquoise stones. The "squash blossoms" charms on the neck strands and the central "naja" pendant are typical features of Navajo jewelry made in the 20th century.

This silver bird pendant measures only 1¼″ by 2″. Blue turquoise is used to represent the animal's eye and stomach.

A cast-silver bracelet decorated with geometric stamped designs and five polished turquoise stones.

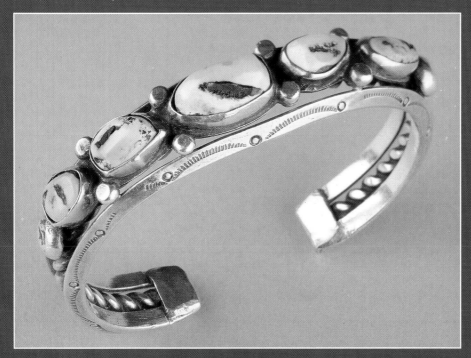

A wrist guard made of leather and silver inset with turquoise and porcelain. Navajo bowmen traditionally wore wrist guards to protect their arms from bowstrings.

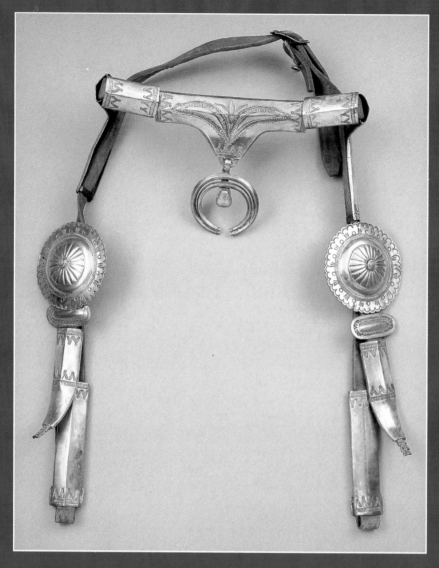

A belt made from seven silver conchas strung on a strap of leather.

A silver headstall for a horse. The two discs (conchas) rested on the animal's cheeks, and the naja pendant rested on its forehead.

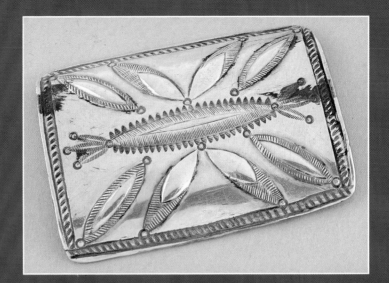

A silver belt buckle decorated with etched designs.

A silver tray with stamped designs. The Navajos often decorate objects sold to tourists with images that are not traditional but are perceived as "Indian" by whites.

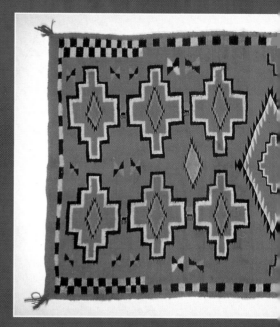

A 20th-century Navajo rug made with commercial dyes. Non-Indian customers often prefer the bright colors produced by artificial pigments.

A serape made between 1850 and 1875, the Classic Period of Navajo weaving.

This serape was woven in the Transitional Period (1875–90), during which the Navajos adapted their weaving traditions to satisfy the demands of the tourist market.

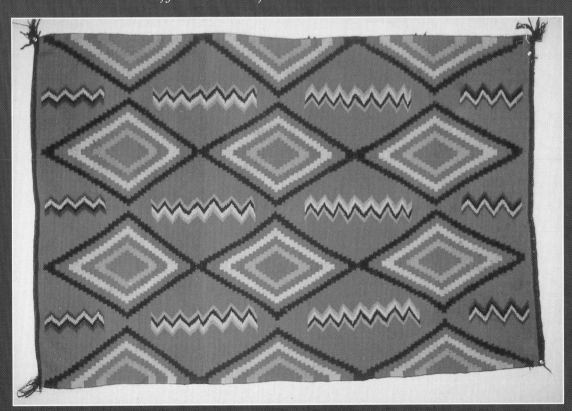

The pattern of horizontal stripes on this "chief blanket" has long been a favorite of Navajo weavers.

A woven saddlebag decorated with tassels, probably made in the early 20th century.

continued from page 32

ey. With the little they did spend on the Navajos, they bought a small amount of spoiled food. Without proper nourishment, many Navajos became ill at Fort Sumner.

Soon, many non-Indians realized that Carleton's program was unsuccessful. Some thought that the plan was unjust; others thought it was costing the government too much money. In September 1866, General Carleton was relieved of his command. At this time, the government became especially concerned about its dealings with Indians. The first transcontinental railroad, one that would link the West to the East, was almost complete. Previously, settlers had gone west by wagon. By train, travel would become easier and faster. Soon, even more settlers would probably journey west. Before they arrived, the government wanted to make peace with all Indians along the railroad. The U.S. Indian Peace Commission, a group made up of military men and civilians, was formed to do the job. In 1868, two of its members, Colonel Samuel F. Tappan and General William Tecumseh Sherman, visited the Navajos at Fort Sumner.

The 2 commissioners met with 10 Navajos who had been chosen to represent the tribe. General Sherman told them that the Navajos could go to another area known

as Indian Territory (now the state of Okla-
homa) or return to their homeland. If the Navajos returned to their homeland, though,
they would have to live peacefully in a
clearly defined area. The Navajos said they
wanted to go home, then signed a treaty
with the U.S. government.

The treaty defined the boundaries of Navajo country, which became known from
then on as the Navajo Indian Reservation. It
also required the U.S. government to assign
teachers to Navajo children and to give
seeds, farming equipment, and livestock to
the Navajo people. The Navajos had to allow roads, railroads, and military posts to
be built on their land. They also had to prom-
ise not to raid non-Indian settlements.

As bad as their dealings with the U.S.
government had been, the Navajos knew
that other Indian tribes had suffered more.

*Navajos build
quarters for U.S.
troops at Fort
Sumner while armed
soldiers look on.*

Some had lost much of their land to the United States. Others were forced to leave their homelands and permanently move to other areas of the country.

Because the Navajos were allowed to come home to the land within the four sacred mountains, it was easier for them to return to their way of life. Barboncito even predicted that the "corn (would) grow in abundance and everything (would) look happy." However, they experienced many hardships. Because they had a season of bad weather, many of their crops produced small harvests. Some people went hungry. Also, other tribes were raiding the Navajos, and the government was not providing the protection it had promised them in the peace treaty. The government did, however, send livestock to the Navajo people and assign a teacher to the Navajo children.

The land that the Navajos had been given, though, was only part of their original homeland. As their population grew and their livestock multiplied, the Navajos sought to regain more and more of the land that had been theirs before the Long Walk. Most of this land was not being used by non-Indians, so the federal government returned some of it to the Navajos. However, the government also created a Hopi Indian reservation on a portion of the territory the

Navajos wanted back. The Hopis and Navajos were expected to share the area. Later, this arrangement caused problems between the two tribes.

The reservation became a home to others as well. In the late 19th century, trading posts began to take root on Navajo land. They were among the few places for miles and miles where Indians could trade goods with non-Indians. The posts also became social centers where people gathered to talk and visit one another.

The Navajos traded crops or raw wool for coffee, flour, fabric, or metal pots. Sometimes, the Indians had nothing to barter, however. Then, traders gave them goods anyway in exchange for a *pawn*. A pawn was some valuable object. If a Navajo paid back a debt, the trader returned the pawn. If the Navajo did not, the pawn became the trader's property.

The Navajos would often leave their woven blankets or jewelry as pawns. Soon, the traders found that non-Indians were interested in obtaining these items. They encouraged the Navajos to start making blankets, rugs, and jewelry not just for themselves, but also for trading.

The traders were very influential. They asked the Navajos to weave blankets with the designs that appealed to most customers. Weavers also learned to make rugs, because non-Indians often requested them.

The traders also affected the design and crafting of jewelry and other silver items. They encouraged Navajo men to become masters at silversmithing, a skill the Navajos had learned from Mexicans decades before the Long Walk. One trader, Lorenzo Hubbell, brought Mexican silversmiths to the reservation to help the Navajos become even more skilled. The Navajos learned to use Mexican and U.S. coins to make belt buckles, necklaces, earrings, bracelets, buttons, horse bridles, and many other items. Traders also brought turquoise to the reservation. By the 1890s, the Navajos had begun setting this bluish stone into their jewelry.

In the late 19th century, Navajo culture was influenced by yet another institution—Christianity. Presbyterian missionaries had arrived on the reservation in 1869. Mormons, Catholics, and members of the Christian Reformed church soon followed. Although the missionaries came to the reservation primarily to convert the Indians to Christianity, they also built schools. Many of the priests became interested in Navajo culture. The Catholic school, called St. Michaels Mission School, became a center for

the study of Navajo language, religion, and way of life.

A U.S. government agency, the Bureau of Indian Affairs (BIA), had provided the Navajos with a school and erected several more in the late 19th century. There were also off-reservation boarding schools, such as Carlisle Industrial Training School in Carlisle, Pennsylvania. However, these federal schools aimed to assimilate Indians into American society with no respect for Navajo values.

This group of young Navajos were photographed six months after arriving at the Carlisle Industrial Training School.

Most of the teachers at the BIA schools did not stay long enough to learn about Navajo culture. Usually, they taught in English and did not allow the use of the Navajo language. As a result, Navajo parents tended to choose mission schools for their children. In fact, they were very much opposed to the BIA educational system. Sometimes when attendance officers came to take children to a public school, parents would bar the door of their hogan.

In the 19th century, the Navajos suffered many intrusions from the outside world, but sometimes they benefited from such contact. They were forced to make decisions as a people, instead of individually. This caused the Navajos to become more politically unified, laying the foundation of the Navajo Nation.

The Long Walk was probably one of the first incidents that helped to shape the Navajo people into a nation. The United States had treated the Navajos as one people, so the Navajos began to see themselves as one people. They began to understand the need to work together to survive. Soon, however, they learned that in order to truly act as one people they needed to be organized. ◣

*Eroded Navajo land,
photographed in the
early 20th century*

CHAPTER 4

Watching Over the Homeland

In 1921, an exciting discovery was made on Navajo land. Oil was found buried deep beneath the soil, and several oil companies were eager to strike a deal for the rights to drill on the reservation. The Navajos were very pleased because a deal with an oil company could bring in a considerable amount of money to the tribe. One problem stood in the way, though: The oil companies could not determine with whom they should negotiate.

Traditionally, the Navajos did not have just one leader who spoke for the whole tribe. It would surely be difficult for them to choose one now. There were many communities on the reservation, and each one had a different opinion about renting the land to be drilled for oil. If the tribe had to choose one leader, everyone would want the leader to come from their area. It was clear that if all the tribespeople's opinions were to be represented, the Navajos would have to elect a group of leaders.

A tribal council was established. It was composed of 12 people called delegates, who would make decisions affecting all Navajos. On July 7, 1923, the Navajo Tribal Council met for the first time and elected Chee Dodge as its chairman. As chairman, Dodge would be responsible for running council meetings. The council then began to discuss how to negotiate with the oil companies interested in drilling on Navajo land. It decided to rent the land and to demand a portion of the profits. The money would go into a general tribal fund to be spent on programs and projects that would benefit all Navajos. This decision was made in keeping with the traditional Navajo value of helping the tribe as a group.

The tribal council was such a success that the Navajos decided another type of organization was needed to deal with local, day-to-day problems. Beginning in 1927, small communities organized into *chapters*. The chapters elected officers to settle minor disputes, such as arguments between Navajo families. Also, representatives from the chapters helped keep the Navajo Tribal Council informed of what was happening in their area of the reservation. In this way, the council kept in touch with the concerns of all the Navajo people.

In 1928, a representative of the federal government came to talk to the council about a problem that concerned all Navajos. He told the council members that the tribe's livestock was destroying its land. The region was poorly supplied with water. To find water, the animals usually had to travel very far. Along the way, they grazed on grass, often eating it down to its roots and exposing the soil. Strong winds and flash floods then carried the topsoil away. Wide gaps and gullies covered the countryside. This process, known as *erosion*, made the land difficult to farm.

The U.S. official offered a solution. He told the Navajos that they should get rid of some of their sheep, horses, goats, and cattle. With fewer animals, less of the land would be grazed and trampled, and erosion would be less of a problem.

The Navajos did not agree with the federal government. Instead, they believed that the government needed to increase Navajo territory so that the animals would have more land on which to graze. Also, they thought that waiting for a little more rain would be better than getting rid of their animals. The area had been stricken by drought, and the lack of moisture had helped to erode the soil.

The Navajos needed to convince not only federal officials but also the non-Indian population of Arizona and New Mexico that the tribe needed more land. The borders of these states, formed in 1912, contained part of the Navajo reservation and the public lands that the tribe wanted to obtain. The non-Indians, however, already had plans for this public land. They hoped to see the territory used for such projects as Boulder Dam (later renamed Hoover Dam). The dam was to provide water for farms, control floods, and produce electric power throughout the entire Southwest. The senators and congressmen elected by the non-Indian population tended to share their views. So, the Navajos had little chance to acquire more land.

The tribe refused to give up hope, especially after the appointment in 1932 of John Collier as the commissioner of Indian affairs. Collier had become interested in Indian life while traveling in the Southwest in the 1920s. As commissioner, he wanted to help all Indians across the United States. He introduced many programs at the Bureau of Indian Affairs that supported Indians' rights.

Likewise, Collier wanted to help the Navajos solve their soil erosion problem. However, he was not familiar with the Navajo way of life. He did not know that sheep were traditionally given to singers for presiding over ceremonies or to children so that they could learn Navajo values and responsibilities. Like other U.S. officials, Collier believed that getting rid of some animals was the best way to help the Navajos.

Collier first tried to bargain with the Navajos. He promised to convince the government to grant the Navajos more land, as well as more local schools, federal jobs, and water development. In return, the Navajos had to reduce their livestock. However, Collier was able to secure only very small additions to the reservation.

Even though the Navajos felt that Collier had not met his part of the bargain, they cooperated with the federal government. The Navajo Tribal Council voted that all herds should be reduced by 10 percent. However, after 1936, the government decided that this was not enough. Government agents started forcibly taking animals away from

their owners. According to Navajo stories, sheep and horses were seized and killed, left lying on the land to rot. The Navajos were outraged. After fighting agents or refusing to round up their herds, many went to jail.

As their herds diminished, the Navajo people found it more and more difficult to make a living solely by raising livestock. Some took jobs in towns off the reservation. Although these jobs helped them make a living, working off the reservation disrupted

Government agents in 1940 round up Navajo horses to be killed.

the Navajo way of life. Children were not raised in the traditional way because adults were no longer able to stay at home.

The Navajo culture was affected in other ways as well. The loss of their animals had made their world unbalanced. Traditional religious leaders were asked to restore the world to its former order, but their ceremonies could not stop the interference of non-Indians in Navajo affairs. As a result, many Navajos turned to other religions.

The 1930s were a difficult time for all Navajos. Many of their animals had been taken away, and with them, the Navajos' traditional way of making a living. The tribe's relations with the United States grew worse than ever. Among themselves, too, harmony had been disturbed. Indeed, in the coming years, the Navajos would struggle to keep their culture alive. ▲

*Three Navajos who
served in the military
during World War II*

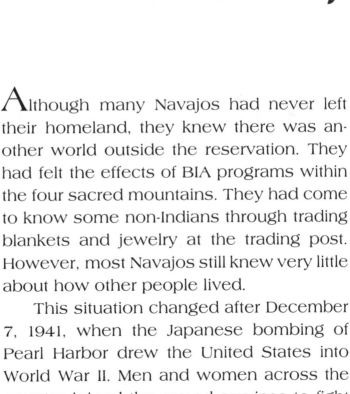

CHAPTER 5

Their Dual Identity

Although many Navajos had never left their homeland, they knew there was another world outside the reservation. They had felt the effects of BIA programs within the four sacred mountains. They had come to know some non-Indians through trading blankets and jewelry at the trading post. However, most Navajos still knew very little about how other people lived.

This situation changed after December 7, 1941, when the Japanese bombing of Pearl Harbor drew the United States into World War II. Men and women across the country joined the armed services to fight the Axis Powers, which comprised German,

57

Italian, and Japanese forces. At the same time that many Americans left their jobs to go off to war, war-related industries expanded. Uniforms, weapons, and ammunition had to be made. The Navajos, like many other minority groups, were given new opportunities. Navajos found jobs working in Arizona at an ordnance depot, a place where military supplies were kept. They also worked in the sugar beet fields in Colorado and Utah and for the railroad. Some picked cotton in Texas and lettuce in Arizona. For many Navajos, this was their first wage-earning job and first time off the reservation.

The Navajos were not only reaping a greater income, though. They were committed to the war effort. Both men and women entered the armed services and traveled to foreign lands. They served in Europe and fought against the Japanese on islands in the Pacific. In the Pacific, however, Navajo soldiers played an especially important role in the U.S. war effort. The Americans needed a code to communicate secret messages. Phillip Johnston, the son of a missionary, thought of a solution. His father had worked on the Navajo reservation for many years, so Johnston was familiar with the Navajo language. He thought the language could successfully be used as a code because it was so complex. The Japanese could not easily decipher it.

Soon after Johnston presented his idea to the Marine Corps, the 382nd Platoon was formed, composed solely of Navajo volunteers. These Navajos became known as Codetalkers. The Codetalkers had to make up new names for weapons and war goods because there were no words for these things in their language. For instance, they called dive-bombers—airplanes that drop bombs—*ginitsoh*. Ginitsoh actually meant "sparrow hawk." The way a dive-bomber charges downward toward its target reminded the Codetalkers of the way a sparrow hawk in flight dives toward its prey.

The enemy was never able to break the code, and the Navajo Codetalkers became heroes. They were seen as special soldiers, symbolizing the Native American commitment to the United States. To honor them, a large statue of a Codetalker was erected in Phoenix, Arizona, in 1989.

The Navajos who supported the United States in the war effort did so because they saw themselves as both Navajo and American. As well as being committed to their tribe, the Navajos felt allied with other

The 1989 dedication
of the statue
representing a
Navajo Codetalker

people in the United States, even though they had been mistreated by the federal government in the past.

In some ways, the Navajos benefited from their efforts in the war. Not only did the war provide many Navajos with their first job, it also exposed them to different cultures. The experience altered their view of the world.

All Navajos certainly wanted their own culture to survive. None thought of themselves as just American. They were Navajo Americans. Many veterans, however, came to believe that it would be a good thing for the Navajo people to have more contact with the outside world. To do this, they believed, the Navajos needed a better education, especially a better command of the English language. Veterans also wanted the tribe to be more forceful in its dealings with the federal government.

The first thing the Navajos did was to hire a lawyer. Tribal chairman Sam Ahkeah chose Norman Littell, a former U.S. assistant attorney general, to represent the Navajos in the tribe's legal disputes with the United States. Littell was the Navajos' lawyer for 20 years. During that time he advised the tribe to develop its government and its economy.

Littell represented the Navajos in court, but the Navajos themselves went before Congress to testify to the urgent need for improved roads, schools, and health care. In 1950, Congress passed the Navajo-Hopi Rehabilitation Act, which called for funds to be given to the Navajos over a period of 10 years. With this money the Navajos were able to improve reservation roads and highways and to build more schools.

As roads were improved, travel became easier. Navajos could shop at places other than the local trading post. Tourists could more easily visit the reservation. Even the development of industries on the reservation seemed possible. The Navajos were no longer so isolated from the rest of the country.

Navajo children could more easily attend school, too. In the past, when families made a living by raising livestock, children were needed to help tend the family herd. Now, many adults had jobs, so their children had the time to go to school. Not all of them were able to enroll, however. There were not enough BIA and mission schools near the reservation for all the new students. The BIA tried to provide the students a place in the local schools. It set up trailers on the reservation where more classes could be held. Still, even more schools were needed.

Many of the children who could not find a place in local schools traveled far away to BIA boarding schools. Some children even attended non-Indian schools off the reservation and lived in dormitories built by the tribal council. With the changing attitude to-

Navajo children in a trailer school on the reservation in 1958

ward education after the war, however, this situation was unsatisfactory to Navajo parents. They were becoming more concerned and wanted to be more involved in their children's education. The Navajos needed a public school system on the reservation so that there would be plenty of schools and the children would not have to travel far to attend them.

Public schools are funded by state governments through state taxes. The states in which the Navajo reservation was situated, however, refused to finance schools for the tribe's children. The Navajos, as residents of federal Indian reservations, were not required to pay state taxes. The state governments, therefore, saw no reason to pay for the Navajos' schools.

Luckily, the U.S. government stepped in. In 1953, Congress agreed to fund a public school system on the reservation. Many more Navajo children were then able to attend school and return home to their families at the end of each day.

Not all funding for the Navajos' projects came from the federal government, however. Other funds became available in the 1950s when more oil was discovered on Navajo lands. Millions of dollars came into the tribal treasury each year. Also, *uranium*, which had been mined on the reservation during the war, continued to add to the tribal fund. Uranium is a metal used to make atomic bombs and to fuel nuclear power plants. As interest in atomic energy grew after the war, the Navajos took in more and more money from mining uranium.

Because tribal funds were steadily increasing, the Navajos were able to improve the quality of reservation life. A college scholarship program was created. A newspaper, called the *Navajo Times*, was founded. Buildings for chapter meetings were constructed, and the Navajo government was expanded.

These and many other developments after the war strengthened the Navajo people economically, politically, and culturally. In the decades to follow, the Navajos would continue their effort to become independent of federal funding and assert their pride in being Navajo Americans. ▲

The Ned A. Hatathli Culture Center is located on the campus of Navajo Community College, the first community college to be built on an Indian reservation.

CHAPTER 6

A Nation of Navajos

By the end of the 1960s, the future looked much brighter for the Navajos. Reservation life was getting better all the time. More schools, staffed by Navajo teachers, were being built on the reservation. More jobs were available closer to home as industry developed nearby. The amount of money in the tribal treasury grew larger and larger. The Navajo people had indeed laid a strong foundation for independence. In 1969, the tribal council resolved that the people should officially call themselves the Navajo Nation.

Despite all these changes, the Navajos continued to observe many of their ancient ways. They realized that they had to learn to deal more effectively with non-Indian peoples, but they did not wish to live exactly like the non-Indians in American society. No matter what, they were Navajos, and they wanted to live as Navajos.

To make sure their children learned about Navajo culture, the Navajos insisted that some local schools teach students about the old ways. One such school, called Rough Rock Demonstration School, opened in 1966. It emphasized Navajo history, culture, and language. Also, the school's Navajo Curriculum Center published books written in both Navajo and English. These texts drew upon traditional Navajo stories, such as that of Changing Woman and her twin sons.

More and more Navajo adults started attending colleges and universities. Some returned home to work as teachers. Navajo teachers at reservation schools became good role models, inspiring Navajo students to study hard.

A tribal scholarship fund helped many Navajos go away to college. Not every student wanted to leave the reservation, though. For them, the tribal council founded the Navajo Community College (NCC) in 1968. It was the first community college on an Indian reservation. Navajos could earn associate degrees or they could enter NCC's arts and crafts programs. Even today, Navajos can study to become skilled silversmiths at NCC. So traditional crafts have not been completely abandoned for other professions.

Another organization that helped the Navajos in the 1960s and 1970s was the Office of Navajo Economic Opportunity (ONEO). ONEO, established in 1965, developed many new programs to help Navajos improve their life. One program helped them form small businesses. Another aided Navajos in search of better housing.

ONEO also provided a legal service called Dinebeiina Nahiilna be Agitahe (DNA), which is Navajo for "attorneys who contribute to the economic revitalization of the people." Before DNA was created, few Navajos who needed a lawyer could afford to hire one. Now, with DNA's staff of 18 attorneys, any tribesperson could get legal advice.

The federal government funded ONEO's programs, but Navajos ran the organization. The first head of the ONEO was Peter MacDonald. MacDonald had been one of the youngest Codetalkers during World War II. After the war he earned a degree in electrical engineering and worked for six years as

a project engineer with Hughes Aircraft. However, he returned to the reservation in 1963 to work for the tribal government.

For five years he directed ONEO's programs, most of which helped many Navajo people. When he ran for tribal chairman in 1970, he was very popular. He easily defeated his opponent, Raymond Nakai, who had served one term as chairman.

Several issues were important to the Navajo people at the time of the election. First of all, the Navajos sought to develop industry on the reservation. However, they disapproved of how Nakai had gone about doing this. In the early 1960s, Nakai had negotiated contracts with several companies. He allowed one to strip-mine some land for coal and another to construct an electricity-generating facility and a power plant on the reservation. The strip-mining had destroyed the land, and the burning of the coal had polluted the air. This hurt the reservation's tourist industry. Even worse, it caused the Navajos to feel that, in exchange for a little money, they were ruining the homeland for which their ancestors had fought so hard.

Peter MacDonald, the first Navajo to head the Office of Navajo Economic Opportunity (ONEO)

Another issue that greatly concerned the Navajos at this time was their joint use of land with the Hopi Indians. Since 1882, the Hopis had lived on a reservation surrounded by Navajo land. The two tribes had long argued over where their animals could graze. Now they also bickered over who could live on this land and who should benefit from oil revenues. The Hopis took the matter to the courts and won exclusive rights to this area of land. The Navajos felt sorely defeated. Because of this loss, longtime Navajo attorney Norman Littell was dismissed. As tribal chairman, one of Peter MacDonald's first moves was to hire new legal counsel.

On the whole, the MacDonald administration took a more aggressive approach to governing the Navajo Nation. It focused on areas such as education, housing, and labor. In 1971, it created the Navajo Division of Education. This organization established a teacher education program so that more Navajos could train to become instructors. The Navajo Housing Authority (NHA), also created by MacDonald's administration, built and managed tribal housing. MacDonald also boosted the economy by developing the Navajos' natural resources. He was able to renegotiate gas and oil leases so that the Navajos would reap a higher profit.

MacDonald's success inspired some Navajos to be more assertive. Many people opened their own small businesses. The Navajos were so pleased with the job MacDonald had done that they reelected him in 1974. Some critics, however, were not impressed by the chairman. They claimed that the Navajos' situation had not really improved during MacDonald's first term.

Even more damaging to his reputation was a scandal that surrounded the NHA. The federal government accused an NHA official of misusing tribal funds. After he pleaded guilty, MacDonald was also brought to court on similar charges. The jury, however, was unable to reach a verdict in his case.

Still popular, MacDonald was reelected to a third term in 1978. Four years later, however, he lost the race for chairman to Peterson Zah. MacDonald remained popular in some chapters and was able to defeat Zah in the 1986 election to win a fourth term as tribal chairman.

Soon, MacDonald came under attack again by both Indians and non-Indians. He was accused of having illegally spent tribal funds on himself. In early 1989, he was sus-

pended by the tribal council. Finally, on October 22, 1990, MacDonald was sentenced to 5 years and 335 days in jail and fined $11,000 by Navajo judge Robert Yazzie.

Despite the scandals surrounding Peter MacDonald and his administration, the Navajo Nation has emerged as a political and cultural entity. The Navajos continue to improve their educational system, develop their economy, and strengthen their government. At the same time, while striving for self-determination, the Navajos respect the old way of life. Within the four sacred mountains, many Navajo Indians still practice traditional ceremonies, speak the Navajo language, and tell the many stories that relate the experiences of their people. ▲

A young Navajo girl, photographed in Monument Valley, Arizona

CHRONOLOGY

ca. 1500	After a long period of migration from northern North America, Navajo Indians become residents of what is now the American Southwest
1849	Skirmish with the United States after U.S. troops kill Navajo leader Narbona
1863	Surrender to U.S. troops and go on the Long Walk to Bosque Redondo Reservation
1868	Sign treaty with U.S. government and return to their homeland, now an offical reservation
1921	Discover oil on the reservation
July 7, 1923	Navajo Tribal Council holds first meeting
1932	John Collier becomes commissioner of Indian affairs; era of livestock reduction begins
1941	Navajo men and women volunteer to defend the United States in World War II
1965	Navajos establish the Office of Navajo Economic Opportunity (ONEO) and appoint Peter MacDonald its executive director
1969	Officially call themselves the Navajo Nation
1970	Elect MacDonald chairman of the Navajo Tribal Council
1989	Tribal Council suspends MacDonald
Oct. 22, 1990	Navajo judge Robert Yazzie sentences MacDonald to 5 years and 335 days in jail

GLOSSARY

Blessingway rite a traditional ceremony in Navajo religion performed to promote *hozho*

chantway a Navajo ceremony performed by a singer to heal or protect a person

clan a large group of people who have a common ancestor

culture a specific set of beliefs, values, and behaviors of a group of people

drypainting a picture formed on the ground with crushed charcoal and sandstone, used in Navajo ceremonies to heal the sick; also called a sandpainting

hogan a cone-shaped home with a frame built from logs and bark and covered with a thick coat of mud

hozho the Navajo word meaning "harmony, happiness, beauty, and goodness"—the values the Navajos strive to attain in their world

kinaalda the ceremony performed for a Navajo girl when she reaches puberty

reservation a tract of land set aside by treaty for the occupation and use of Indians

INDEX

INDEX

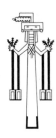

ABOUT THE AUTHOR

LEIGH HOPE WOOD holds a B.S. from Emory University and an M.A. in American studies from New York University. She is an editor and writer who lives in New York City.

PICTURE CREDITS

AP/Wide World Photos, pages 60, 70; BIA/Milton Snow Collection, Navajo Tribal Museum, Window Rock, AZ, pages 54–55; Culver Pictures, pages 48–49; Department of Library Services, American Museum of Natural History, pages 23, 38 (top [neg. # K13015], bottom [neg. # K12638]), 39 (bottom [neg. # K12640]), 40 (top [neg. # K12894]); Photo by Richard Erdoes, pages 66–67; Photo by Eric Kroll, pages 74–75; Library of Congress, pages 2, 16, 20–21, 24–25; Michael Latil Photography, courtesy Smithsonian Institution, pages 33 (cat. # 362001), 34 (cat. # 404068), 35 (top [cat. # 422580], bottom [cat. # 362.031]), 36 (top [cat. # 361.525], bottom [cat. # 165466]), 37 (top [cat. # 361.982], bottom [cat. # 404082]); Museum of the American Indian, page 40 (bottom); National Archives, page 42; Native American Painting Reference Library, private collection, pages, 6, 11; Smithsonian Institution, pages 28, 46; UPI/Bettmann Archive, pages 56–57, 63

Map (page 14) by Gary Tong

i970.3
WOO
Wood, Leigh Hope
The Navajo Indians

468313

$13.95

DATE		

CHILDREN'S DEPARTMENT
INDIAN BOOKS
7 DAYS ONLY
NO RENEWALS

OCT 2 3 1992